Space Robots

BY KIRSTEN W. LARSON

AMICUS HIGH INTEREST • AMICUS INK

Amicus High Interest and Amicus Ink are imprints of Amicus
P.O. Box 1329, Mankato, MN 56002
www.amicuspublishing.us

Library of Congress Cataloging-in-Publication Data
Names: Larson, Kirsten W., author.
Title: Space robots / by Kirsten W. Larson.
Description: Mankato, Minnesota : Amicus High Interest/
  Amicus Ink, [2018] | Series: Robotics in our world |
  Audience: Grades 4 to 6. | Includes index.
Identifiers: LCCN 2016041972 (print) | LCCN 2016051592
  (ebook) | ISBN 9781681511474 (library binding) | ISBN
  9781681521787 (pbk.) | ISBN 9781681512372 (ebook)
Subjects: LCSH: Space robotics–Juvenile literature. | Robotics-
  -Juvenile literature. | Space probes–Juvenile literature. | Outer
  space–Exploration–Juvenile literature.
Classification: LCC TL1097 .L37 2018 (print) | LCC TL1097
  (ebook) | DDC 629.43–dc23
LC record available at https://lccn.loc.gov/2016041972

Editor: Wendy Dieker
Series Designer: Kathleen Petelinsek
Book Designer: Tracy Myers
Photo Researcher: Holly Young

Photo Credits: inhauscreative cover; NASA/JPL-Caltech/
WikiCommons 4-5; Elena Duvernay/Stocktrek Images, Inc./
Alamy Stock Photo 6; Wuka/Dreamstime.com 9; NASA/JPL-
Caltech 10; MR1805/iStock 13; Xinhua/Alamy Stock Photo
14-15; Triff/Shutterstock 17; NASA/SpaceX/WikiCommons
18; NASA/Expedition 39/WikiCommons 21; Gary I
Rothstein/EPA European Pressphoto Agency B.V./Alamy Stock
Photo 22; Catmando/Shutterstock 24-25; NASA/JPL-Caltech/
University of Arizona/Cornell/Ohio State University 26;
NASA/JPL-Caltech/WikiCommons 28-29

Printed in the United States of America

HC 10 9 8 7 6 5 4 3 2 1
PB 10 9 8 7 6 5 4 3 2 1

Table of Contents

Robots in Space

In 2012, a space robot landed on Mars. Success! Scientists around the world want to know more about Mars. But going there is a dangerous job. A **rover** like *Curiosity* is just the robot for the job. For more than four years, this robot has been cruising around Mars. It drills into rocks with its robotic arm. It studies the dust. Then it tells people on Earth what the rocks are made of.

Mars rover *Curiosity* is like a moving science lab.

Rosetta dropped *Philae* to the comet's surface in 2014. *Rosetta* kept flying.

 What did we learn from the *Rosetta*?

Before *Curiosity*, scientists sent many robots into space. Think of sending people on a 10-year trip to land on a speeding comet. No, thanks! Instead, *Rosetta* launched in 2004. On its trip, it studied other comets and planets. In 2014, it met up with the comet. One part of the robot landed on the speeding rock. *Rosetta* continued to circle in space. They sent pictures and information to Earth.

 Lots! It sent photos to Earth. We could see the size and shape of the comet. We also learned about the frozen gases on the comet.

Going to Space

Before robots could go to space, we needed a vehicle to take them there. We needed rockets. In the 1940s, people built rockets that flew into outer space. Lift off!

In 1957, a Soviet R-7 rocket launched the first **satellite**. *Sputnik* circled Earth every 100 minutes. It was not a robot. But it started a space race. Who could get to space next? Soon, many people and robots blasted into space.

 Did the Soviets invent rockets?

An artist's drawing shows what *Sputnik* might have looked like as it circled Earth.

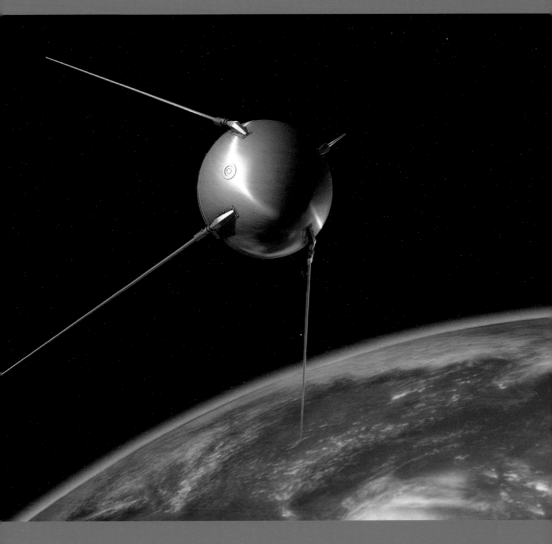

 No. In AD 1200, Mongols packed bamboo tubes with gunpowder. A soldier lit it on fire. The flaming arrow shot itself to the enemy!

Mariner 2 was the first robotic spacecraft. It sent information about Venus to Earth.

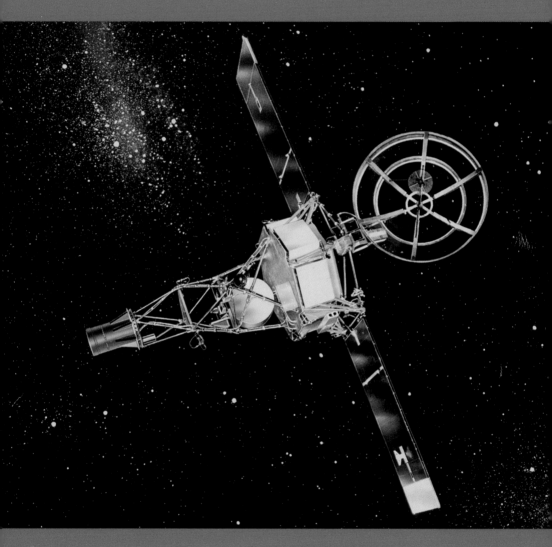

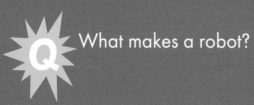 What makes a robot?

Mariner 2 was the first robot in space. NASA sent it soaring past Venus in 1962. It studied particles from the Sun. It looked at space dust. It studied Venus's clouds and surface.

Mariner 2 could do work by itself. It had a computer to tell it what to do. The computer weighed 11.5 pounds (5.2 kg). Today's laptops weigh half that.

Robots can sense, plan, and act. **Sensors** gather data. Computers make decisions. They can make mechanical parts move.

In 1969, people landed on the Moon. Nothing lived there. Could there be life on Mars? NASA needed to find out. Two *Viking* spacecraft blasted off in 1976. Each *Viking* had two parts. The **orbiter** circled Mars. Meanwhile, the **lander** fell away. Its rockets fired, and it flew toward Mars. Parachutes slowed it down. Computers controlled the landing. Touch down!

 Has anyone been to Mars yet?

People call Mars the Red Planet.
Space robots have learned about
the red dust on Mars.

 Not yet. Scientists need to create new
spaceships. They need to learn the best way
for people to live there for many months.

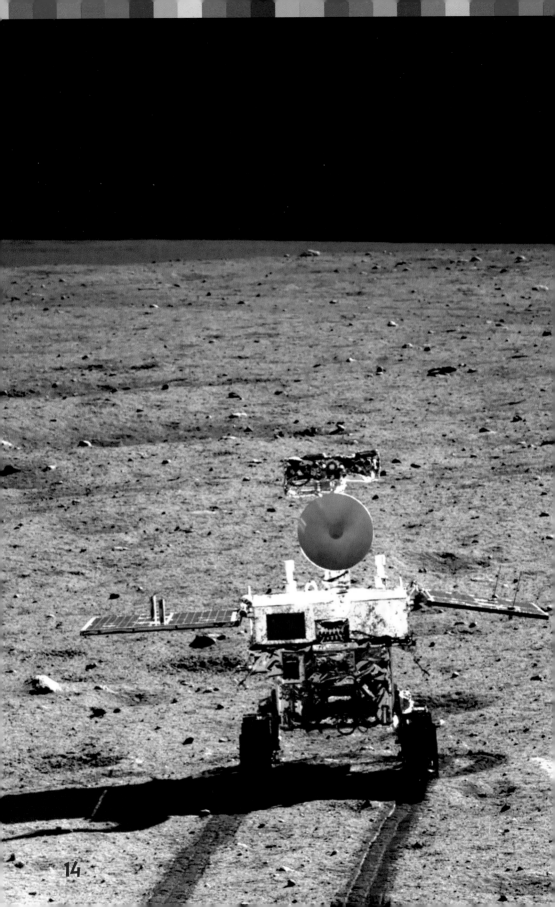

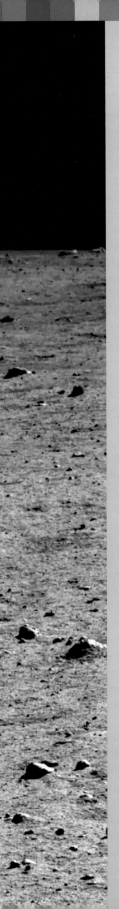

Space Robots at Work

Scientists study space in many ways. Probes are sent to faraway planets. Rovers have cruised on the Moon. These machines need power to run. But they don't use normal batteries. Some rovers like *Yutu* used solar power to work on the Moon. Solar panels collect the sun's rays. They turn the sunlight into power.

Yutu **explored the Moon's surface from 2013 to 2016, powered by solar panels.**

15

Today's space robots make many decisions on their own. In 2003, NASA sent the rover *Spirit* to Mars. It drove around taking photos. It looked at soil. At night, *Spirit* sent photos to Earth. In the morning, scientists looked at them. They planned the rover's next job. They instructed the rover to go to a new place. *Spirit* decided the best way to get there. Off it went.

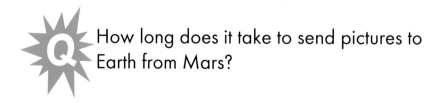
How long does it take to send pictures to Earth from Mars?

Giant dishes on Earth send and receive information from space robots and other spacecrafts.

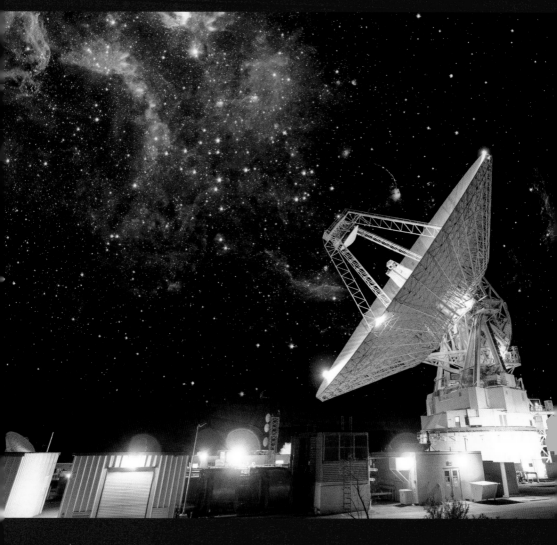

 About 20 minutes. This is how long commands from Earth take too. Space missions can be slow.

The *Dragon* takes supplies to astronauts at the space station.

 Q What if something goes wrong while the *Dragon* tries to connect to the ISS?

Some space robots fly. These spacecraft are **drones**. They have no pilot inside. The *Dragon* takes supplies to the International Space Station (ISS). Computers drive the craft. **Radar** tells the drone where it is and how fast it is going. Rocket thrusters on the drone fire. They move the drone into position. The drone connects to the ISS by itself.

 No problem! Astronauts at the ISS can steer the drone. They can use remote control.

The ISS is a giant machine. It sometimes needs new parts. Astronauts have to go outside of the ISS on a **spacewalk**. It is a dangerous job. Today robots like Dextre and Canadarm 2 help. They can fix things. They can change parts. Now astronauts don't need to do as many spacewalks. They have more time for science.

Dextre is connected to the end of the Canadarm2. These two robots unpacked the *Dragon* on their own.

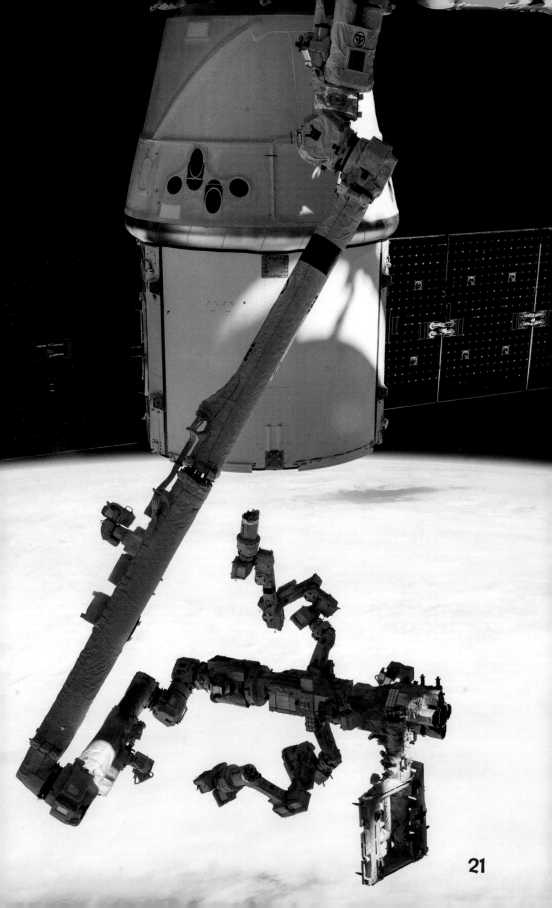

Someday human-like robots may work side-by-side with people in space. At the ISS, NASA is testing a **prototype**. It is called the Robonaut. Its fingers bend just like yours. For now, astronauts are making sure it works in space like it does on Earth. Someday, it might do spacewalks on its own.

Scientists tested Robonaut 2 on Earth before sending it to the ISS in 2011.

What Comes Next?

In the future, we will see all types of robots. NASA is working on robot subs and helicopters. Subs could explore the sea on Titan, Saturn's largest moon. The sub would send information back to Earth. Helicopters could skim the skies of Mars. They would find new places to explore. Then they could guide rovers.

This art shows what a view of Saturn might look like from its moon Titan.

25

A rover spent two years studying this crater on Mars. A more robotic rover might do it faster.

 Q Why should robots do more things on their own in space?

New technology means rovers could do more jobs by themselves. They could act more like a person than a tool. First, 3D cameras would snap pictures of the land. Then, computers would compare the new pictures with those stored in the rover's computer. The computer would look for new rock textures or colors. When the rover finds something new, it would automatically go to that place to explore.

 It is faster. If a robot could decide the next step, it wouldn't have to wait for commands from Earth.

Out of This World

Space is a harsh place. But some people think we could live there. We need to learn more. So we will need to keep making robots. Making these advanced robots takes many years. NASA started work on Robonaut 20 years ago. It is still just a prototype. How much longer until it's finished? No one knows.

This art shows what a future probe to Jupiter's moon Europa could look like.

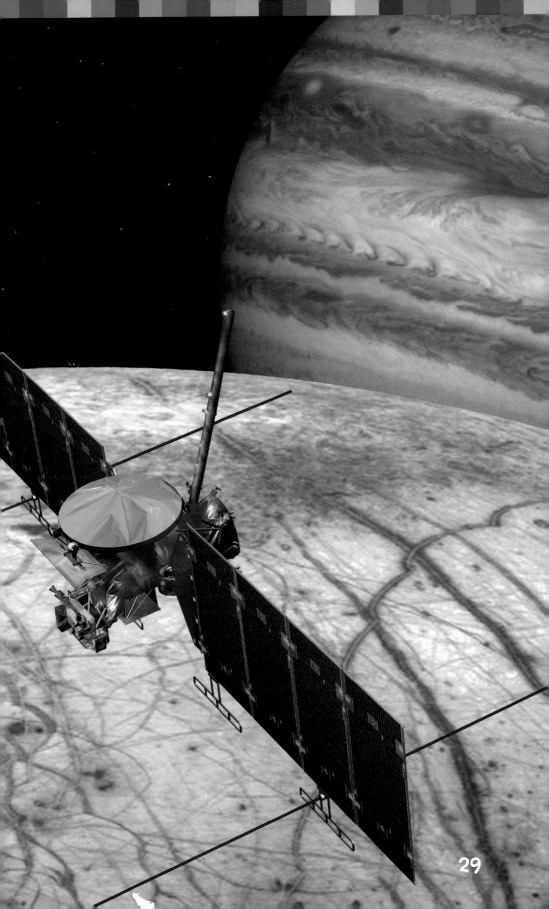

Glossary

drone An aircraft that does not need a pilot; also called an unmanned aerial vehicle (UAV).

lander A spacecraft that lands on a planet, moon, comet, or other space body.

orbiter A spacecraft that flies around a planet, moon, or other space body.

prototype An early version of a new invention built to see if it will work.

radar A way some vehicles find their way by bouncing radio waves off of objects.

rover A robot that drives on the surface of a planet, moon, or other space body.

satellite A spacecraft that circles around the earth or some other space body.

sensors An instrument on a robot that takes in information.

spacewalk When an astronaut wears a space suit and goes outside of the vehicle or station to do a job while floating in space.

Read More

Furstinger, Nancy. *Robots in Space*. Lightning Bolt Books. Robots Everywhere! Minneapolis, Minn.: Lerner Publication Company, 2015.

O'Hearn, Michael. *Awesome Space Robots*. Mankato, Minn.: Capstone Press, 2013.

Stewart, Melissa. *Robots*. Washington, D.C.: National Geographic, 2014.

Websites

ESA Kids: Life in Space
http://www.esa.int/esaKIDSen/LifeinSpace.html

NASA's Mars for Kids
http://mars.nasa.gov/participate/funzone/

NASA's Robotics Multimedia
http://www.nasa.gov/audience/foreducators/robotics/multimedia/#.V0iPkZMrKRs

Index

About the Author

Kirsten W. Larson is the author of more than 20 books for young readers. She used to work with rocket scientists at NASA, but now she writes about science for kids. Her favorite robots are NASA's *Curiosity* Mars Rover and LEGO Mindstorms. She lives near Los Angeles, California. Learn more at kirsten-w-larson.com.